70.09.2017

To Ami,

Don't ever give up on
your dreams and always
believe!

D1743961

From Inspiring Vanessa

The 5 Secrets to Public Speaking Success

Written
By Inspiring Vanessa

Contents Page

Testimonials

Introduction – My Story

Chapter 1 - What's your Why and your Purpose ?

Chapter 2 – Do you have 100% Confidence?

Chapter 3 – Be YOURSELF!

Chapter 4 – Don't be a boring Speaker

Chapter 5 – Speaking from your heart

<u>TESTIMONIALS</u>

I remember the first time someone invited Inspiring Vanessa to come and speak at my event and I was not sure what to expect from a 9 year old!

The energy that came out of this girl when she opened her mouth captured the whole crowds attention straight away while she continued with her motivational teachings she had the crowd join her on an emotional roller-coaster laughing and crying all the way through.

I realised in that moment " I have to sign her right now" and make sure her message is spread around the world.

Vanessa is a true blessing to this world, her wisdom way beyond her years, an old soul waiting to get out there to change to world for better.

Eric Ho – United Kingdom
International Speaker, Entrepreneur, Philanthropist, Educator and Best Selling Author
www.erichoofficial.com

Vanessa is one of the most inspiring young ladies in the entire world. We met her at an event in London. She impacted us with her positive attitude, passion for life, respectful manners and her powerful story. Vanessa wrote master piece book that every kid on the planet must read now.

I am so impressed with the wisdom of Vanessa and her drive to share her inspiring story. Having raised a young author myself and experiencing the excitement of the release of Caleb's first book, I am so happy for Vanessa and her mom Veronika. These two angels are going to make such a huge difference in a very special way.

Matt Maddix – Florida,USA
Public Speaker, Author, dad to Caleb Maddix, Life Coach, Business Consultant
www.mattmaddix.com
Caleb Maddix – age 14
International speaker, Author of Keys to Success for Kids

From the first day I met Vanessa, I knew she was someone special. She has been raised a lover which has led to a burning desire to share that love with the world.

Vanessa speaks with such passion and conviction which empowers adults triple her age and every conversation is one of positivity and the need for growth.

It is not everyday that you see a ten year old artist and a motivational speaker travelling around the country to speak on some of the biggest stages. She has a gift, a gift to transform your thoughts through her words and her art.

Charm Lawrence - UK
Founder Just Be Inspired
www.justbeinspired.com

There is a large group of us in the world who desire to motivate masses of people and then a very small collective of change agents who were born to touch, move and inspire people to action.

Inspiring Vanessa not only lives up to her name but has an infectious energy that influences the influencers to higher levels. It's a joy to know her and even greater joy to serve by her side.

JuVan Langford - California
Men's Empowerment Coach, International speaker and mentor

As her name suggests it, Inspiring Vanessa is nothing short of inspiring! She has a way with words that make you question if you really knew yourself. She is living, breathing proof that age is just a number and if you have the courage to pursue your dreams they you will reap the rewards.

At the age 10 she has unmatched gravitas on stage that captivates every single person in the audience.

I highly recommend everyone to reads this book by Inspiring Vanessa and learns the key steps to take their life to the next level.

Marium Zulfiqar – UK
Intenational Speaker, Mental Health and Child
Abuse Activist and Govt Advisor

In my great honour to be asked to write this foreword.

I travel the world teaching Public Speaking and Communication Skills to people of all ages and backgrounds and I can say with absolute certainty that Vanessa is the most gifted speaker I have ever met!

Vanessa's dedication to learning and developing her skills is very inspiring. Every time I see her perform I am blown away by how easy she makes it look. This is what happens when preparation meets opportunity. When you work that hard behind the scenes, the only option is to be successful.

If you are looking to improve your Public Speaking skills or to increase your confidence, then this is the book for you!

If you get the opportunity to see or learn from Vanessa in person,then definitely take it!

Vanessa's future is incredibly bring! I can't wait to see what she decides to do!

Luke Scott - London
International Speaker and Mentor

Vanessa has a heart felt story, which is close to my heart as I also grew up with only having one parent. She has an ability to stay focused whilst sharing her story inspiring and motivating children and adults alike.

From the first time that I saw her on stage I knew that she was special, telling her story in a funny and unique way, and when she lost her train of thought she brought it back with character which make her stand out.

Vanessa is a wonderful speaker and I look forward in watching her journey unfold.

Laura and David Helen - London
Authors of Amazon Best Selling Book, 3 Steps to Family, Making family important again

Vanessa is a great friend, who is very funny and makes me giggle.

We started speaking around the same time and did some training together. We have shared the stage at some incredible events along side some real superstars.

I know Vanessa will really make a difference to so many kids, she is really inspirational!

Tegan Helen – age 8 – London
Princesspreneur, Speaker and Author of Money for Kids and The Power to Unlock your dreams

Vanessa is a speaker who is one of a kind.

She doesn't just speak,but she has the ability to engage any audience through her powerful story, charisma, and being present and if you don't know Vanessa now, you will do.

Warren Inspire Ryan – London
International Speaker, Mindset Coach and Founder of the Fearless Speaker Academy

Vanessa exhibited at both our summer and winter Ultrakids business fairs. She was a massive hit with the attendees and the VIP's were hugely inspired by her motivational canvases.

Her determination and steadfast ability to stay at the course is a lesson to adults and children alike.

She will no doubt go on to inspire and motivate around the world and myself at the team at Ultra Education are fully supportive of her journey.

Julian Hall - London
"Ultrapreneur", Founder of Ultra Education
www.ultrakids.com

THANK YOU

I would like to say a huge thank you to all the amazing people who wrote the testimonials, they are truly heart warming, and it means a lot.

I would also like to give a huge, huge thank you to my mum for helping me with this book, typing it up, staying up late,showing me what is right and what needs to be changed. Showing me that anything is possible and making my dreams come true.

I love you mum!

My question is what would you like to achieve?

Thank you for reading this book and following my journey, I look forward to meet you.

FOLLOW your dreams
and
live the life you were born to live!

Love from Inspiring Vanessa,age 10

INTRODUCTION
- MY STORY

My story started off when I was born in August 2006. I was a very joyful girl and quite cute . As from 4 years to now I still love art and drawing , because it's my passion . But in 2008 everything changed ..... My Dad left me and my mum, yet I still think about it today . It was a very hard time for me and my mum especially . However , we both knew we had to stay happy we had each other .Have you ever grown up with one parent ? If you do , I understand and it can be quite hard to overcome these type of things , even though for most people there's nothing you can do . But the reason why people don't overcome these things is because they focus on the person about why they did what they did or did they want to and all of these thoughts but meanwhile they focus on the other person's story and not YOURS !

Years past and in 2016 our lives changed . One day , my mum told me that she was going to meet a motivational speaker , his name is Warren Inspire Ryan . A couple months later we finally met him after watching him on the screen all the time .

On that very day something hit me , I realised that wouldn't it be amazing if I could inspire and motivate children and adults all around the world . After I had spoken on that stage for the very first time I continued which allowed me to write this book that you are reading . My credibility grew to a whole new level which led me to meeting Jairek Robbins , Eric Thomas , Eric Ho and Caleb Maddix and many more ! Later on I met Eric Ho in September 2016 and I attended their first event for kids and I was a speaker and ever since then he has helped me with so many things so THANK YOU ERIC!

Quote:
"YOU ARE THE HERO OF YOUR OWN STORY"
-Joseph Campbell

CHAPTER 1

WHAT IS YOUR WHY AND YOUR PURPOSE ?

The first secret is finding your why . Now what is a "why" you may ask .Well a why is your reason or your purpose of why you're being passionate about what you do . Here's an example : A lady is speaking because her why is helping and empowering young women to believe in themselves and to stand up for themselves .

Your why has to be bigger than yourself and your family. Let's say that it's someone's dream to win an Oscar , now that is bigger than themselves and their relatives ! But it NEEDS to be important to YOU ! Who cares if being a chef is who your parents want you to be ! It all starts with you . There's no point of having that why because it's not going to make you work harder or make any difference !

PURPOSE :

Now your purpose can be like your blueprint. Your blueprint is your identity ; who you were born to be. Unfortunately, many people in this world suffer because they followed their parents footsteps.

My mum always says ; "Our children are like sponges, so whatever they see you or hear you doing, they will copy".

It's important for us as children to be surrounded with positive people and those we can learn from.

MY WHY:

My why is to meet Ellen DeGeneres because she helps people and makes people happy, which is a very important element in life

My purpose of speaking is -well, you might of seen in the introduction, but I loved the idea of making an impact on other people's lives, so my journey began in March 2016.

My goal is to inspire children and others to be themselves, have courage and be who they want to be!

Ask yourself these questions :

1. What do people come to me for?

2. What is my passion? (many people end up doing something they don't like)

3. What would I like to do when I grow up? (if your a child or a grown up)

These questions could be a possible topic or subject to talk about during a speech.

The best speakers talk about their experiences and what they've been through. Which can help you to connect with others and have a sort of bond.

Many people focus on money in the career of being in speaking. But if you focus on the money you won't get money as you need to focus on the value. The VALUE you give to other people is more important that the money.

Quote:
" CHANGE YOUR FOCUS, FROM
MAKING MONEY TO SERVING MORE
PEOPLE. SERVING MORE PEOPLE
MAKES THE MONEY COME IN"
-Robert Kiyosaki

CHAPTER 2

DO YOU HAVE 100% SELF-CONFIDENCE?

The second secret is self-confidence. Now self-confidence is a feeling of trust in one's abilities, qualities and judgement.

Self-confidence is a very big step in speaking. Don't worry if you don't have 100% because I am going to teach you some of my tips to improve your confidence.

STEP 1 – Self – belief
It all start with self-belief and you need to believe in yourself before anybody else can believe in you. If you believe you can you are half way there.

STEP 2 - Practice, practice, practice

Personally, my experience was not perfect first, but are we ever perfect?
When I spoke for the first time, I was shaking and horrified. Trust me it was not my best speech and

that's ok because with practise and doing it over and over again, you will get better. You will not be perfect the minute you start because more you practice then more you get comfortable.

This is so, so important because "practise make perfect".

Unfortunately you are not going to be on the same level as Les Brown or Tony Robbins.

The reason why they are well-known speakers is because they worked hard and practised.

If you don want to go on a real stage, then stand on your bed, lay your teddies and toys out and speak!

STEP 3 - Self-esteem

Self-esteem is one of the most important things. If you would like to become a speaker or improve you need to compliment yourself.

Speaking is about helping and empowering. You can't be telling other that they need to be kind to themselves if you are not doing it with yourself.

I hope all those tips are helpful and remember if you believe that you can it become true and if you believe that you can't then that will also become true!

Quote:
"BELIEVE YOU CAN
AND
YOU ARE HALF WAY THERE"

CHAPTER 3

BE YOURSELF!

This is one of the most important things in speaking and also in life. Being yourself!

Now, in the process of being you I guarantee you that your environment is going to change. Here are three things that are going to change in your journey of finding yourself.

1. Judgement
2. Surround yourself with "green"lighters
3. Mindset

1. Judgement can be one of the hardest things in speaking. I hate to say it, but your WILL loose some friends in the process of being yourself. Yes it will be hard and I know exactly how it feels but its ok. I am going to share this with you if you are struggling right now...

When I first shared my business and what I was doing at my school, many things have changed...

For me I felt like I was being treated differently because of what I do. People around me will start to act a bit different, I would say judgemental. I found it quite hard because I love what I do and was very desperate to get my friends back.

Please don't be desperate it pushes people away more. Don't be selfish though,trust me, its very rare that you're the only person who's being judged.

EVERYONE, goes through it but what most people do, is they let that to hurt them.

2. Surround yourself with "Green" lighters.

You are probably thinking what who are green lighters and what they need to do with speaking. Well green lighters are the encouraging and supportive people in your life.

Red lighter on the other hand are people who are exact opposite (discouraging and unsupportable people)

HERE is a little experiment for you :

a) Figure out who are our green and red lighters.
b) How many green's do you have?
c) How many red's do you have?
d) What do you do to get/earn more green lighters?

EXAMPLE:

A lady is going out with her "friends" but they are all NEGATIVE!

Now, do you think she's going to be developing a negative or positive attitude?

The answer is – negative, because she's just using her time sucking up the negativity with her friends,like a vacuum.

However there is a positive side to your surroundings (there's is always a choice). If you surround yourself with successful people, you will be successful. Because of that, you will start developing the same mindset as your role models.

3. Mindset

Mindset is most important tool you will need in the journey of being a speaker.

What is mindset? Well, mindset is a set of thoughts, beliefs and attitudes about yourself and life.

Which determines your behaviour, quality of life and the success that holds in your business (in this case – speaking)

I hope these tips helped you to understand and were helpful, least you know what to expect. Sometimes it can feel like being yourself is almost forbidden.

Yes if you try to be yourself there will always be someone to tell you that who you are is not good enough, but here is the thing - " you cannot fail by being you". One day when you are rich and famous they will be the ones who will remember you.

Now this message is very important. Not only you should be yourself but you should also be different to others, well you need to be odd one to be number one (guess what?) number ONE is an ODD number.

I would highly recommend these books as I have read myself and they helped me and still helping with my journey, success, being myself etc.

1)   Rich Dad, Poor Dad by Robert Kiyosaki

This book teaches you about the stages of money and as it says by Robert himself "what the rich tell their children about Money"

2)   Chicken Soup for Kids (Audible)

I highly recommend to listen to this audiobook because it teaches you about more about kindness and their focus in to really make them kind people

3) Keys to Success for Kids by Caleb Maddix

Key to success teaches your about the big golden nuggets you need to learn in order to get to your success. This book is awesome and I know the author personally – Caleb Maddix (testimonial in the front of the book)

4) Money for Kids by Tegan Helen

When I read this book I was astonished, especially to know that it was written by a 7 year old Tegan Helen, she is probably the most clever 7 year old I have ever met. This will really teach you about your prospective of money.

5) The Power (audio)

The Power for me really shifted my viewing of things. I have learned about the Universe and of cause law of attraction. I highly recommend to listen or read this book.

6)   The Secret (audio)

Before I started my journey of speaking, the first inspirational book was the Secret. This completely amazed me. I found really interesting how other people see their lives and especially their purpose.

Quote:
**"BE YOURSELF –
EVERYONE IS ALREADY TAKEN!"**
- Oscar Wilde

CHAPTER 4

DON'T BE A BORING SPEAKER

I believe and I have learned that entertainment is a must in speaking. You need to speak with passion but people wont listen to you if they are half a sleep. Every 7 minutes your audience wonder off.

Here are some helpful tips and tricks to be the most entertaining speaker others have never heard off.
1. Eye contact
2. Engage with the audience
3. Body language
4. Stand tall
5. Use the space around you
6. Finish with a punch line

1) Eye contact can be the key of having a bond with others. Why? Because its not going to give you as much power by looking at everybody then actually looking directly in someone's eyes. It will give you an emotional attachment. When you looking at someone directly they will feel like you are talking

only to them.

2) Engage with audience

When you engage with the audience it keeps them interested in what you have to say.

Here are some fun things you can do:

a) Do a fun exercise for example ask them to high five the person next to them or put your hand up and say "YES"

b) Ask questions. For example "Ask me why?" and "raise your had if you know how I feel"

c) Stick on a joke. For example (my personal joke) "Why is a vision board called a vision board?" the audience replies -" I don't know", "because you put vision on a board!" Well did you enjoy this one? Everybody wants a laugh!

3) Body language

Your actions speak louder then what you say.

If someone has an upset face, you straight away know that they are sad but if they tell you " I am ok" you are less likely to believe them. Well its the same with speaking. If someone says they're confidence coach but their body language says opposite, unlikely they will get loads of clients.

4) Standing tall is a sign that what you are about to say is going to blow the audience. Be calm. If you are really tense your mind will automatically go BLANK, just be yourself.

5) Use the space around you, the stage is yours. It is very important because if you are all the way back it doesn't give you as much power as standing in the front of the stage. Of cause not too much in the front otherwise you can fall.
Walk proudly on the stage during your speech. But don't walk too fast (they are not watching tennis match, haha) Trust me I was doing it so I am speaking from my own experience, and yes its not the best.

Can I share a short story with you?

The day I was being given my " Young inspirational person " award, I had the most beautiful dress, my hair done and it was at the Bafta in London. I had planned a speech and the whole presentation. But I was only walking too fast.
My mum is usually behind the camera and recording my speeches, however it was quite difficult to film me that time. Well we all learn from our mistakes and I am happy to be sharing it with you.
So when you are walking during your speeches

make sure to stay in one place for about 50 seconds then you walk slowly to the other side and make sure you are using eye contact. You can also change it a bit if you have slides or writing on the flip chart.

6) Finishing with the punch line (for example a quote or a message) will close your speech in a high level. A quote or a message needs to be powerful, something for your audience to take away with them.

I believe that all those tips and tricks will help you on your journey of public speaking.

When you are a speaker, you are a teacher, people not only see you and hear you, most importantly FEEL YOU.

Here is a method I have learned from Warren Inspire Ryan. This is called the 4 E's.

1. *Entertain*
2. *Engage*
3. *Educate*
4. *Empower*

All of these 4 E's are used by some of the biggest speakers around the world.

Quote:
"YOU NEED TO BE ODD
TO BE NUMBER ONE "
-Inspiring Vanessa

CHAPTER 5

SPEAK FROM YOUR HEART

You may ask what does it mean to speak from your heart, when you are speaking from your heart you flow.

It is a fact that you don't need to prepare day and night. For me personally, let say if its an event holding about 100 people, I would write down 3 points then memorise them and fill them in word by word while I am on stage. If its an big event (around 300 people and more with top class speakers) I will prepare my presentation in more detail and I will create my own slides too.

Once you are comfortable on stage you can use these tips to structure your speech;

1) Find a subject
2) Write 1-3 points
3) Smash it!

1) Find the subject.

In my opinion I base it on which event I will be speaking at. If it's a personal development event, then I would speak about mindset and personal development. How to accomplish dreams, how to stay focused, self -love etc.

2) Write 1-3 points

What does it mean? It means to write at least 3 simple point to talk about. If I was going to talk about public speaking I would write points lie this:

Name of the speech:
- Practice,practice,practice
- Communicate
- When you feel like quitting think of the reason why you started.

As simple as that! Was this useful?

3) Smash it!

Then all you have to do is put all your passion and excitement into you speech. Many people have a FEAR of public speaking (if you do) use the fear and put that into the speech.

FEAR – False Evidence Appearing Real

Did you know that people fear more public speaking then death? Add emotion into your speech. Like I said before speak from the heart people can feel the emotion and that way your speech will be more powerful and inspiring.

Speaking with passion means that your audience feels you, they can relate to you and what you are saying and they are interested. Its something that they WANT to learn You need to put life and energy into your hands.

My question to you is do I teach something interesting or necessary? If the answer is no, that you need to start packing your knowledge up and putting it out there. If you don't you won't get the same results that you would like.

In March 2017 I have launched my first every audio book and its called *"The 12 Keys to Success"* and if you would like to learn more please visit my website. Please find all social media and how you can find me or contact me at the back of this book.

Quote:
**"ANYONE CAN ACHIEVE
THEIR DREAMS BUT ONLY
IF THEY HAVE THE COURAGE
TO ACCOMPLISH THEM"**
- Inspiring Vanessa

FIND OUT MORE :

Website and audio book - www.inpiringvanessa.com

Follow me on all social media and let me know what you liked the most.

Youtube – www.youtube.com/inspiringvanessa
Twitter – www.twitter.com/inspiringv10
Instagram – www.instagram.com/instagram
Snapchat - @vinspires
Facebook – www.facebook.com/inspiringvanessa

contact me – vanessa.sam6@gmail.com

NOTES:

NOTES:

NOTES:

NOTES:

NOTES:

Printed in Great Britain
by Amazon